A CENTURY *of*
GLASGOW

Many famous ships were built on Clydeside. The *City of New York* was made in John Brown's Clydebank yard at the end of the nineteenth century. Riveting was a skilled job, and aided by a 'hauder on' who held the rivet from the other side. Here, the double hull was being constructed. (*UGA*)

A CENTURY *of* GLASGOW

BRUCE DURIE

SUTTON PUBLISHING

First published in the United Kingdom in 2000 by
Sutton Publishing Limited · Phoenix Mill
Thrupp · Stroud · Gloucestershire · GL5 2BU

British Library Cataloguing in Publication Data
A catalogue record for this book is available from the British Library.

ISBN 0-7509-2655-4

Front endpaper: Glasgow Green, *c.* 1904. (*ML*)
Back endpaper: View from Kelvingrove Park, Glasgow University at Gilmorehill. (*ML*)
Half title page: Statue of St Mungo, Kelvingrove. (*ML*)
Title page: Miller's House, Northwoodside, *c.* 1900. (*UGA*)

 Published in association with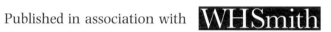

Thanks to my parents,
Dave and Frances Durie, and my son, Jamie,
for their support, encouragement and tolerance
of the authorial process.

Typeset in 11/14pt Photina.
Typesetting and origination by
Sutton Publishing Limited.
Printed in Great Britain by
The Bath Press, Bath.

Contents

James Macintyre's engraving of Glasgow Cathedral shows the Adam-designed Royal Infirmary (1794) beside it. The cathedral itself originally had two towers to the west, demolished in the 1840s to make it more harmonious with the surrounding architecture.

Britain: A Century of Change

Two women encumbered with gas masks go about their daily tasks during the early days of the war. (*Hulton Getty Picture Collection*)

The sixty years ending in 1900 were a period of huge transformation for Britain. Railway stations, post-and-telegraph offices, police and fire stations, gasworks and gasometers, new livestock markets and covered markets, schools, churches, football grounds, hospitals and asylums, water pumping stations and sewerage plants totally altered the urban scene, and the country's population tripled with more than seven out of ten people being born in or moving to the towns. The century that followed, leading up to the Millennium's end in 2000, was to be a period of even greater change.

When Queen Victoria died in 1901, she was measured for her coffin by her grandson Kaiser Wilhelm, the London prostitutes put on black mourning and the blinds came down in the villas and terraces spreading out from the old town centres. These centres were reachable by train and tram, by the new bicycles and still newer motor cars, were connected by the new telephone, and lit by gas or even electricity. The shops may have been full of British-made cotton and woollen clothing but the grocers and butchers were selling cheap Danish bacon, Argentinian beef, Australasian mutton and tinned or dried fish and fruit from Canada, California and South Africa. Most of these goods were carried in British-built-and-crewed ships burning Welsh steam coal.

As the first decade moved on, the Open Spaces Act meant more parks, bowling greens and cricket pitches. The First World War transformed the place of women, as they took over many men's jobs. Its other legacies were the war memorials which joined the statues of Victorian worthies in main squares round the land. After 1918 death duties and higher taxation bit hard, and a quarter of England changed hands in the space of only a few years.

The multiple shop – the chain store – appeared in the high street: Sainsburys, Maypole, Lipton's, Home & Colonial, the Fifty Shilling Tailor, Burton, Boots, W.H. Smith. The shopper was spoilt for choice, attracted by the brash fascias and advertising hoardings for national brands like Bovril, Pears Soap, and Ovaltine. Many new buildings began to be seen, such as garages, motor showrooms, picture palaces (cinemas), 'palais de dance', and ribbons of 'semis' stretched along the roads and new bypasses and onto the new estates nudging the green belts.

During the 1920s cars became more reliable and sophisticated as well as commonplace, with developments like the electric self-starter making them easier for women to drive. Who wanted to turn a crank handle in the new short skirt? This was, indeed, the electric age as much as the motor era. Trolley buses, electric trams and trains extended mass transport and electric light replaced gas in the street and the home, which itself was groomed by the vacuum cleaner.

A major jolt to the march onward and upward was administered by the Great Depression of the early 1930s. The older British industries –

textiles, shipbuilding, iron, steel, coal — were already under pressure from foreign competition when this worldwide slump arrived. Luckily there were new diversions to alleviate the misery. The 'talkies' arrived in the cinemas; more and more radios and gramophones were to be found in people's homes; there were new women's magazines, with fashion, cookery tips and problem pages; football pools; the flying feats of women pilots like Amy Johnson; the Loch Ness Monster; cheap chocolate and the drama of Edward VIII's abdication.

Things were looking up again by 1936 and new light industry was booming in the Home Counties as factories struggled to keep up with the demand for radios, radiograms, cars and electronic goods, including the first television sets. The threat from Hitler's Germany meant rearmament, particularly of the airforce, which stimulated aircraft and aero engine firms. If you were lucky and lived in the south, there was good money to be earned. A semi-detached house cost £450, a Morris Cowley £150. People may have smoked like chimneys but life expectancy, since 1918, was up by 15 years while the birth rate had almost halved.

In some ways it is the little memories that seem to linger longest from the Second World War: the kerbs painted white to show up in the

A W.H.Smith shop front in Beaconsfield, 1922.

blackout, the rattle of ack-ack shrapnel on roof tiles, sparrows killed by bomb blast. The biggest damage, apart from London, was in the south-west (Plymouth, Bristol) and the Midlands (Coventry, Birmingham). Postwar reconstruction was rooted in the Beveridge Report which set out the expectations for the Welfare State. This, together with the nationalisation of the Bank of England, coal, gas, electricity and the railways, formed the programme of the Labour government in 1945.

Times were hard in the late 1940s, with rationing even more stringent than during the war. Yet this was, as has been said, 'an innocent and well-behaved era'. The first let-up came in 1951 with the Festival of Britain and there was another fillip in 1953 from the Coronation, which incidentally gave a huge boost to the spread of TV. By 1954 leisure motoring had been resumed but the Comet – Britain's best hope for taking on the American aviation industry – suffered a series of mysterious crashes. The Suez debacle of 1956 was followed by an acceleration in the withdrawal from Empire, which had begun in 1947 with the Independence of India. Consumerism was truly born with the advent of commercial TV and most homes soon boasted washing machines, fridges, electric irons and fires.

The *Lady Chatterley* obscenity trial in 1960 was something of a straw in the wind for what was to follow in that decade. A collective loss of inhibition seemed to sweep the land, as the Beatles and the Rolling Stones transformed popular music, and retailing, cinema and the theatre were revolutionised. Designers, hair-dressers, photographers and models moved into places vacated by an Establishment put to flight by the new breed of satirists spawned by *Beyond the Fringe* and *Private Eye*.

In the 1970s Britain seems to have suffered a prolonged hangover after the excesses of the previous decade. Ulster, inflation and union troubles were not made up for by entry into the EEC, North Sea Oil, Women's Lib or, indeed, Punk Rock. Mrs Thatcher applied the corrective in the 1980s,

Children collecting aluminium to help the war effort, London, 1940s. (*IWM*)

A street party to celebrate the Queen's Coronation, June 1953. (*Hulton Getty Picture Collection*)

as the country moved more and more from its old manufacturing base over to providing services, consulting, advertising, and expertise in the 'invisible' market of high finance or in IT.

The post-1945 townscape has seen changes to match those in the worlds of work, entertainment and politics. In 1952 the Clean Air Act served notice on smogs and pea-souper fogs, smuts and blackened buildings, forcing people to stop burning coal and go over to smokeless sources of heat and energy. In the same decade some of the best urban building took place in the 'new towns' like Basildon, Crawley, Stevenage and Harlow. Elsewhere open warfare was declared on slums and what was labelled inadequate, cramped, back-to-back, two-up, two-down, housing. The new 'machine for living in' was a flat in a high-rise block. The architects and planners who promoted these were in league with the traffic engineers, determined to keep the motor car moving whatever the price in multi-storey car parks, meters, traffic wardens and ring roads. The old pollutant, coal smoke, was replaced by petrol and diesel exhaust, and traffic noise.

Fast food was no longer only a pork pie in a pub or fish-and-chips. There were Indian curry houses, Chinese take-aways and American-style hamburgers, while the drinker could get away from beer in a wine bar. Under the impact of television

Punk rockers demonstrate their anarchic style during the 1970s. (*Barnaby's Picture Library*)

the big Gaumonts and Odeons closed or were rebuilt as multi-screen cinemas, while the palais de dance gave way to discos and clubs.

From the late 1960s the introduction of listed buildings and conservation areas, together with the growth of preservation societies, put a brake on 'comprehensive redevelopment'. The end of the century and the start of the Third Millennium see new challenges to the health of towns and the wellbeing of the nine out of ten people who now live urban lives. The fight is on to prevent town centres from dying, as patterns of housing and shopping change, and edge-of-town supermarkets exercise the attractions of one-stop shopping. But as banks and department stores close, following the haberdashers, greengrocers, butchers and ironmongers, there are signs of new growth such as farmers' markets, and corner stores acting as pick-up points where customers collect shopping ordered on-line from web sites.

Futurologists tell us that we are in stage two of the consumer revolution: a shift from mass consumption to mass customisation driven by a

Millennium celebrations over the Thames
at Westminster, New Year's Eve, 1999.
(*Barnaby's Picture Library*)

desire to have things that fit us and our particular lifestyle exactly, and
for better service. This must offer hope for small city-centre shop
premises, as must the continued attraction of physical shopping,
browsing and being part of a crowd: in a word, 'shoppertainment'.
Another hopeful trend for towns is the growth in the number of young
people postponing marriage and looking to live independently, alone,
where there is a buzz, in 'swinging single cities'. Theirs is a 'flats-and-
cafés' lifestyle, in contrast to the 'family suburbs', and certainly fits in
with government's aim of building 60 per cent of the huge amount of
new housing needed on 'brown' sites, recycled urban land. There looks
to be plenty of life in the British town yet.

Glasgow: No Mean Century

In 1900 Glasgow was at the peak of its powers and its fame. From its early days as a favoured site of the Church, it had risen to international prominence as a centre for trade, manufacture and learning. At the turn of the century Glasgow's city administration was hailed worldwide as a model of enlightened control, its municipal and social structures more like those of an Athenian city state than a British Victorian municipality. Birmingham, Sheffield, Manchester and Leeds – Johnny-come-latelies with their nineteenth-century charters – looked on with envy at the Second City of Empire. The 1901 International Exhibition was an exposition of Glasgow's civic pride, its industrial and commercial muscle and its determination to enjoy itself at all costs. But the ensuing century was not so gentle to the 'dear green place' (*Glas Cu*) from which the name Glasgow derives.

Glasgow's history is as long as any of Europe's capitals. There were Neolithic settlements, probably attracted by the equable climate and the well-stocked, readily navigable and easily forded river. The Romans came, made peace with the local Damnonii and established one end of their third great wall in Britain (the Antonine) which marked the north-western edge of their empire. When Rome departed, Christianity stayed – St Ninian visited and the two patron saints, St Mungo and his mother St Enoch, established the first Episcopal church. Glaswegians are still fiercely proud of their patron saints – pointing out that they came from Fife is still as good a way as any to provoke a fight in a Glasgow pub.

By 1175 Glasgow had burgh status, thanks to its role as an important ecclesiastical centre, and in 1490 was granted a charter to export fish (notably smoked or cured salmon and herring) to Europe. Barely 150 years later the first major shipment of tobacco

Isambard Kingdom Brunel wasn't the only engineer to wear a stovepipe hat. Robert Napier, the godfather of Glasgow marine construction, is shown here in the 1850s with his family and foremen. John Elder (far right), his most senior manager, founded his own engineering dynasty. Many other Napier employees established engineering or shipbuilding companies of their own, including Randolph & Elder (with John Elder's son), J. & G. Thomson and Denny & Bros. Napier's own business was marred in his later years by family business squabbles, but his legacy lasted more than 100 years. (*UGA*)

landed on a Glasgow-based vessel from Antigua. The seeds of future commercial prosperity were being firmly laid.

Bishops, and later archbishops, provided the city with its cathedral (twelfth century) and university (fifteenth century). Their reign was every bit as firm as that of the prince-bishops of Durham. It is a mystery why Rowan Atkinson has not spotted the comic potential in Glasgow's first Archbishop, Robert Blacadder (1492). But episcopal power came to an end with the Reformation and in 1689 Glasgow ceased to be a 'bishop's burgh'. The Merchant City became the new reality. It had been described, none too kindly, as 'a fishing village with a cathedral' but was about to exert its already considerable reach.

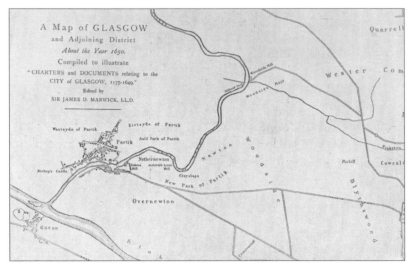

In 1650 Glasgow was still a small burgh but growing fast, with some 12,000 inhabitants. The River Clyde was shallow and narrow at Glasgow which prevented large volumes of river trade. But this was soon to be addressed by those aspiring to create the Merchant City. (*UGA*)

It had grown from a settlement to a sizeable community of 2,000 (with a university) by 1450, doubled that by 1550, risen to 7,000 by 1600, doubled that by 1660 and continued to expand in population to over 75,000 in the nineteenth century while retaining its compact nature.

A large part of the expansion had been due to the burgeoning American trade found possible after the Union of the Crowns (1707) and the removal of draconian English Navigation Laws, which denied Glasgow access to many of the markets and rich sources of tobacco and sugar – not that a bit of judicious smuggling hadn't subverted much of that. Canny political conservatism and continued support for the House of Hanover over the Jacobites preserved this situation until the War of Independence again threatened to decimate Glasgow's trade. The Industrial Revolution came at the right time, and the city took a sharp swerve towards the engineering, shipbuilding and steelmaking which drove its expansion for the next 100 years.

Rennie Mackintosh designed, Greek Thomson dreamed and built, and Harry Lauder sang, and everyone, it seemed, looked to Glasgow for creativity, warmth and good example. Scottish regiments were 'fighting for strangers' all over the world and their civilian cousins were building railways, bridges, canals and telegraphs anywhere the map was pink.

From 1900 Glasgow started growing even faster. Before the First World War everything seemed possible. Life was still hard for many, but work was abundant. They flocked to jobs in factories, foundries, shipyards, mills and shops. New workers came from other parts of Scotland, from Ireland (many of them descendants of Scots sent to 'the plantation' centuries earlier) and from all corners of the Empire – and, strangely, Italy. A look at the name above the door of almost any restaurant, café, ice-cream parlour or delicatessen today bears witness to the remarkable influx and assimilation of Italians into Glasgow's heart.

Up to 1918 Glasgow built ships for trade, for the growing passenger lines and for the Navy, which were the envy of the world. 'Clyde-built' was a synonym for sturdy, level-headed, efficient craft, yet capable of extravagance when necessary – much like the Scots themselves. But this period also saw the rise of thrown-up housing which was to become the tenement slums of Glasgow's shame, and a cheek-by-jowl contrast to the elegance of its West End mansions and its city centre boulevards, shopping streets and municipal buildings.

After the First World War hard times started. The 1920s and the depression of the 1930s hit Glasgow harder than most. The image of No Mean City – razor gangs roaming unsafe streets, Saturday night fights in dance halls and chronic poverty – was more imagined than real, and certainly not general. Yet Glaswegians themselves fostered this image and were quietly proud of it, as they were with the 'Red Clydeside' tag, Keir Hardie and James Maxton. The stolid, unflinching, practical unflappability which built Glasgow's industry is not a stone's throw from the bolshie class warfare that almost destroyed it. Yet 'I Belong to Glasgow' continued to twang the heartstrings.

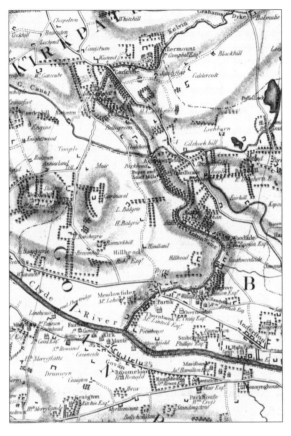

By 1795, on the doorstep to a new century, and after recovering from the loss of trade following American independence, Glasgow was ripe for expansion. Already the river had been opened up and Atlantic trade was a reality. Wealthy merchants and industrialists built houses and expanded the boundaries of the city. (*UGA*)

The 1940s saw a city of a million souls, many of them poorly housed and badly fed. War had, as ever, provided short-term prosperity for industry, but in the aftermath poor judgement denuded the city itself of what made it special – its compact grandeur, its vitality and many of its people. Moved to bland housing estates and 'New Towns' in a well-meant but ill-judged attempt to relieve inner city congestion, many of the younger people whose energy might have led a new industrial and civic revolution found nothing but drab desolation and the feeling that they had been dumped on another planet. Small wonder that many found America, Canada, New Zealand, Australia and South Africa more appealing prospects.

It has taken Glasgow fifty years to find its pride again on the threshold of a new century. Large industry is all but gone. The small businesses which supplied and thrived from it are closed or gone elsewhere. The specialist shops, department stores, theatres, cinemas and dance halls have been replaced by Euro-bars, Irish theme pubs, chrome-and-glass malls and clubs.

The 'dear green place' is gone forever. Urban motorways dissect the city's heart, grey concrete where granite and warm sandstone once pointed proudly to heaven. And the replacement of enlightened but firm civic government with self-interested quangos did little to inspire any feeling of self-worth. But Glasgow has found a new role as a commercial centre, as a merchant city once again, and is prepared to celebrate its architectural and cultural heritage without becoming enmired in nostalgia.

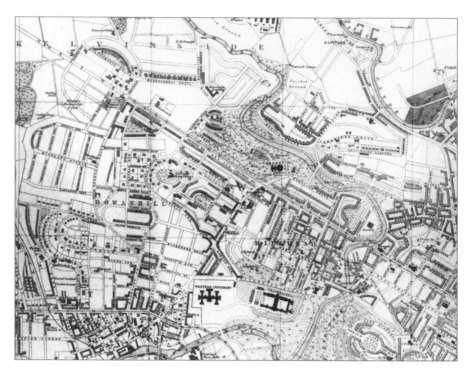

The 1880s were the heyday of building in Glasgow, with elegant Victorian streets laid down in the pattern familiar to today's visitors. (*UGA*)

It is a city of contrasts and contradictions – City of Culture but No Mean City. Home to the tenements of the Gorbals, but City of Architecture and Design. Proud owner of one of the great medical schools, but top of the league for cancer, heart disease and poor dentition. For all its reputation as a town of hard men, Glasgow has been noticeably free of the riots, mass violence and football hooliganism which have marred the recent history of other UK cities.

Some of this is to do with geography. Glasgow made the most of its position near the west coast to be the hub of the early boatbuilding industry, which paved the way for its primacy as a shipbuilding centre. Easy access to the Atlantic and the North Sea provided a commanding position in textiles, tobacco and ships themselves as well as many other finished goods. Although on the same latitude as Moscow to the east and Canada to the west, the climate is gentler than either of those, free of harsh winters and sea ice or sweltering summers too hot to work.

But much of it is owing to local temperament. 'Second City?' one native spiered at me while compiling this book. 'We're second at nothing, pal!' As the common toast goes: 'Here's tae us. Wha's like us? Damn few, and they're a' deid.'

The Start of
the Century

The last farm in the West End was, like much other open land, swept away by Glasgow's expansion. This is now the site of a bowling club so some green remains! (*UGA*)

Between 1870 and the start of the First World War Glasgow was considered one of the finest, richest and most civilised cities in Europe and a model of how a modern industrial society should be organised and governed. Glasgow had more open spaces and parkland than any other European city of comparable size as well as municipal water, gas and a telephone system. Museums, galleries, libraries and other elegant public buildings were erected, including Kelvingrove museum, shown here at the turn of the century. (*UGA*)

The famous Kibble Palace in the Botanic Gardens on Great Western Road is one of Glasgow's greatest buildings. Built by engineer John Kibble at his own home in Coulport, Loch Long, this unique glasshouse was presented to the Royal Botanic Institution in 1873. It was dismantled, shipped up the Clyde and rebuilt, with two new wings off the smaller dome. The building was originally used as a winter garden for concerts and events. The Botanical Collection was started in 1881 when the Royal Botanic Institution bought out the lease. Today the Kibble Palace houses flora from temperate climes. This interior picture dates from 1900. (*UGA*)

Glasgow Green, seen here in a 1904 postcard, has been the city's common land for as long as it has existed, and the citizenry stoutly opposes any plans to make it otherwise. Often a focus for the attention of developers, it has escaped this fate so far. It has always been a place for people's recreation, sport and amenity – including such diverse activities as drying clothes and holding political rallies. In many ways it was, and remains, the heart of Glasgow. (*ML*)

'The People's Palace' was a name commonly given to institutes of popular culture in many European cities at the turn of the century. Despite the egalitarian (even Socialist) sounding name, they were often patrician and paternalistic in tenor. The one on Glasgow Green always was and has remained fiercely populist. This staff portrait is taken in the Winter Gardens, generally supposed to have been built in the shape of HMS *Victory* turned upside down. (*ML*)

St Vincent Street looking west to where it joins Argyle Street, *c.* 1900. (*UGA*)

This is Glasgow at the very height of its wealth, power and optimism. It had come far from its fishing village with a cathedral origins. Until recent times the sea and the rivers were the only sensible way to travel around the west of Scotland. There were few roads and the many hills and inlets made land travel complicated and often dangerous. Therefore a system of ferries, river crossings and inlet traffic developed. Since it was easier to move goods around by water, a merchant fleet was required, alongside the many fishing vessels in operation, and there was also a need for naval protection. This, and the later pleasure craft trade, was the basis for an extensive shipbuilding industry. Originally, boats had been built by intinerant shipwrights who travelled up and down the coast and to the islands, constructing what was needed out of materials to hand. Later, this became formalised in static shipyards. The western part of the Clyde, near the river mouth, is a natural harbour with good, safe inlets for waiting out a storm. The route inland was also there by sailing as far as possible up the Clyde.

The earliest dockyards were at Greenock and Dumbarton, where Robert the Bruce had ships built as early as the 1320s and James IV as late as 1520. However, the Clyde was only of importance to the western coast. The major shipbuilding took place in the Forth and Tay rivers, with their easier access to the European markets via the North Sea. As late as 1730 the Upper Clyde was effectively 'a shallow, narrow salmon stream where cobbles precariously navigated' (Neil Munro, *The Clyde*, 1907). About this time the abundant fishing available off the west coast began to be exploited and John Scott of Greenock started to build herring trawlers from 1711. The Union of the Crowns in 1707 increased Scotland's trade across the

St Vincent Street looking east towards George Square, *c.* 1900. (*UGA*)

Atlantic, particularly in tobacco. This necessitated the deepening of the upper Clyde, and the construction of the Forth–Clyde canal, linking Scotland's two great inland water routes. By 1800 it was not unusual for ships of 100 tons or more to navigate the Clyde up to Glasgow.

American Independence had cut off a ready supply of built ships and timber. This meant more trade for local yards. By then, some of the great shipbuilding companies had been established.

At the same time the textile industry was growing in importance, which not only provided more cargo – raw materials in and finished products out – for the Glasgow shipping companies, but also led to the development of steam power, notably by local boy James Watt. Almost instantly steam engines were brought to bear on shipping, the first commercial steamship, *The Comet*, built in 1812.

Glasgow's increasing prosperity was expressed in its elegant architecture, wide streets and diversity of local services – publicly owned and municipally managed tramways, refuse collection, fire service and police.

It had also become a consumer city with an identifiable white-collar middle class – including female clerks and 'lady operators' for the telephone service – and a professional class consisting of the university dons plus lawyers, doctors and clergy. In 1900, when these photographs were taken, Glasgow was on a par with any major city in Europe or America.

The Clyde was spanned by road bridges. Jamaica Bridge, the second over the river, shown here in 1909, leads to Jamaica Street. The 1751 name is a reflection of the eighteenth-century trade in cotton, rum and sugar, major imports from the New World. The city continued to prosper in the nineteenth century, when the tobacco trade was replaced by textile manufacture, shipbuilding, and the coal and steel industries. This was the site of Lipton's store, famous for its huge cheeses. Lipton, self-styled 'King of the dairy trade', opened his first Lipton Market in Anderston in 1871, selling butter, eggs and ham (his Irish roots showing through) but also own-brand tea and coffee grown in his own Ceylon plantations. In 1881 he bought two 1½ ton cheeses from America, plugged them with half-sovereigns like a plum pudding and advertised the fact widely at Christmas. For years afterwards, buying a piece of 'Jumbo' cheese in the hope of finding riches therein was a Glasgow ritual. (*ML*)

Kelvinbridge on the north side of Hillhead. Great Western Road crosses the River Kelvin, 'Glasgow's other river'. The bridge is lovely at night when it is lit up and the view to the south unusual. Shown here are Lansdowne church and St Mary's church in about 1900–4. (*UGA*)

Royal Scots Greys on parade at Maryhill Barracks. The Scots Greys were raised in 1678 as three independent troops of Scots Dragoons and reformed as The Royal Regiment of Scots Dragoons in 1681. The Greys covered themselves with glory at Waterloo in 1815, by a charge unparalleled in the annals of British or any other cavalry. The appropriate motto 'Second to None' has given place to an eagle, commemorative of the capture of the standard of the 45th Regiment of Napoleon's Invincibles by Ensign Ewart at Waterloo. This picture was taken just after they took part in the last major cavalry charge of the British Army at the Relief of Kimberley during the Boer War. In 1971 they were amalgamated with the 3rd Carabiniers (Prince of Wales's Dragoon Guards) to form The Royal Scots Dragoon Guards (Carabiniers and Greys). (*ML*)

Getting around Glasgow was typically a matter of catching one of the many horse trams which criss-crossed the city. They were known as 'the gondolas of the people' and were cheap – and municipally owned from 1894 (as distinct from private omnibuses). The city owned the tramways. This example is from 1896. (*UGA*)

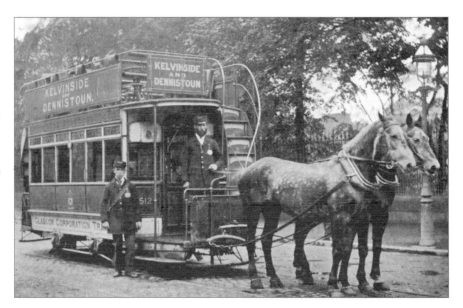

Crossloan (now Clevedon Road) and Great Western Road was an important terminus for horse-drawn trams in 1900. The main routes extended to Queens Park and Kelvinside, where wealthy commuters resided, but also extended to working-class areas and the East End. By this time Glasgow had a restricted underground railway system, a circular route of 7 miles circumference, taking in the shipyards of Partick and Govan. It is known today, semi-affectionately, as the Clockwork Orange – a reference to its small carriages and its corporate livery. The city acquired ownership of the underground in 1923. (*UGA*)

Motorised trams had also largely replaced the horse tram system by 1914, as with this example of the Springfield tram, which ran on the first electrified route in 1898. By 1912 there were over 45,000 employees on the tramways, then the largest department in the Corporation. It also had a reputation for excellent service and for the immaculate turn-out and manners of its staff, enforced by Tramways Manager James Dalrymple. He was something of a local hero and in 1913 contributed over £30,000 to the common good fund out of tramcar income of well over £1 million. He was also famous throughout Europe. (*UGA*)

By the time this picture was taken in 1913 cars had made their appearance on Glasgow's streets, vying for right of way with horsecarts and trams. Motor buses soon followed and this, combined with the railway companies' constant wailing that the tramways' extensions beyond city boundaries was unfair, foreshadowed the demise of the horse and, eventually, the tramcar. (*UGA*)

Shipping, as well as shipbuilding, was a mainstay of Glasgow's prosperity. Here, on a Sunday morning in 1899, Broomielaw berth is full. Vessels identified on the north side include the *Carrick Castle* (formerly *Culzean Castle*), the *Lord of the Isles*, the *Columba* and the *Aggie* (a small coaster chartered by MacBrayne for the Loch Fyne route). On the south sit the *Kinloch*, the *Vivid*, the *Edinburgh Castle* and the *Isle of Arran*. (*UGA*)

In 1901 Lobnitz & Co. and its Renfrew neighbour William Simons built the dredgers which kept the upper Clyde navigable. Here, at least nine are under construction. The Renfrew ferry is in evidence at the top right. (*UGA*)

Glasgow had traded with Japan since the first treaty signed with the West by the Japanese in the time of James VI. In the early twentieth century Japanese industrialists frequently visited Glasgow, eager to learn new techniques and processes. Beardmore's works at Parkhead, more famous today as the home of Glasgow Celtic, made naval guns. The giant steam hammer 'Samson' was said to shake the whole of Parkhead when it pounded night and day. Here a 4,000 ton press is being used to forge the jacket for a 12-inch gun. The skilled forgemasters would shout 'Awa' Parkheid' or 'Awa' Camlachie' to indicate the direction it was to be moved. Japanese visitors who came to learn forge techniques believed these to be some kind of magic incantation necessary for manufacture, and shouted them in their own factories! (*UGA*)

Launch parties were grand ceremonial events with the owners, constructors, contractors and their families and sundry dignitaries attending to see the keel blocks knocked away, the pins withdrawn, the champagne bottle cracked and the drag chains and tugs manoeuvre the vessel from the slipway to the fitting-out yard. This shows Scott's yard at Bowling in 1904 launching the *Foyers*, a steam-driven coastal vessel. (*UGA*)

John Browns started work on Cunard's *Aquitania* in 1911. The first task was to strengthen the slipways before starting work on the keel. New hydraulic riveting machines had been brought into use by then, but still depended on the skills of the riveter to oversee the process. In fact, shipbuilding was a small employer of Glasgow's workforce – less than 3 per cent (but more if Partick and Govan, administratively separate, are included). Metalwork, engineering and forging employed many times more, but much of the output of these boilermakers, coppersmiths, brass foundries and machine shops was taken up by the shipyards. (*UGA*)

By 1906 Beardmore's Dalmuir Works was the largest engine shop in Glasgow and on the entire Clyde. The separate unit in the centre is a brass finishing shop. Beardmore was one of those who came to work with Napier and took over the foundry from him in 1871. His son, William, saw the potential and promise of steel and developed armour plate. Based in the former textile area of Parkhead, William the younger established this yard at Dalmuir in Dunbartonshire, further down the Clyde, and steel mills at Lanark to supply the raw material. (*UGA*)

Coastal steamer *Kenilworth*, *c*. 1900. (*UGA*)

Not all shipbuilding was on a massive scale. Many smaller yards existed which specialised in fishing craft, pleasure boats, lifeboats and other small vessels, like this 1907 captain's steam yacht from the cruiser *Inflexible*, built by Mehan's at Scotstoun. (*UGA*)

The Glasgow Decked Lifeboat Co. of Shettleston also built smaller craft. This picture shows the workers in 1913, unaware that within a year their craftsmanship would be put to a different use, refitting the Navy. (*ML*)

Shipbuilding was not the only industry, and large factories and yards were not the only businesses. This Jewish immigrant had a cap-making factory in the Gorbals in about 1910. This area of Glasgow was truly multi-ethnic: Lewis Grassic Gibbon described it some twenty years later as 'lovably and abominably and delightfully and hideously un-Scottish'. (*ML*)

Other industries which flourished in Glasgow included glass. The works of Barr & Stroud (now part of Pilkington Optronics, and based in Govan) were in Ashton Lane, which has changed from 1900, when this picture was taken, to a trendy pub and restaurant quarter. (*UGA*)

Sadler's Antiques at the corner of Byres Road and Observatory Road (seen here in 1904) catered to the gentry of Hillhead and Kelvinside with money to spend. Presumably they now lodge it with the mortgage company which currently occupies the premises. (*UGA*)

The two Great Exhibitions of 1881 and 1901, both in Kelvingrove Park, displayed Glasgow's pride in its achievements. This picture shows the grandeur of the 1901 exhibition. The gondolas on the River Kelvin attest to Glasgow's Venetian pretensions and James Sellars' Moorish-style building stresses Glasgow's cosmopolitanism. The expressed intent of the 1888 exhibition, smaller in scale than the exercise seven years before, had been to raise funds for a new art gallery and museum. The former opened in 1901 as the centrepiece of the exhibition and cost over £250,000. (*UGA*)

The Prince of Wales (soon to become King) visited the exhibition in the stead of the dying Queen Victoria. The visit underlined Glasgow's growing sense of its own importance – this was justified, since it was now Europe's sixth largest city (after London, Paris, Berlin, St Petersburg and Vienna) and felt equal to all of them. (*UGA*)

Two years later, as Edward VII, he and Queen Alexandra visited Glasgow again. Here they are shown in procession along University Avenue. By this time 'Greater Glasgow' had become more than a political slogan, as the city had had sufficient land added to its boundaries to double its area: the police burghs of Crosshill, Govanhill, Hillhead, Maryhill and Pollockshields, the working-class areas of Balornock, Springburn and Possilpark and – joy of joys to the city treasurers – the well-to-do merchant suburbs like Kelvinside. (*UGA*)

Football, always an obsession with Glaswegians, was dealt a bitter blow in its early days with the Ibrox Park disaster. The collapsed stand at the Rangers home ground in Govan in April 1902 is still remembered. Football had become an organised sport with the establishment of the Football League and the creation of professionalism in 1893. Queen's Park was the first Glasgow club (1867) followed soon after by Rangers (1872) and Celtic (1888, set up as a charity to raise funds for the East End Catholic poor). These two teams took a solidly businesslike approach to the game from the start and, realising that most of their gate money would come from playing against each other, built up the Protestant–Catholic rivalry. Good as a promotional vehicle, it later backfired in the battles of the 1920s and 1930s, with sectarian razor gangs aligning themselves with team support. (*ML*)

It is often said that what marks Glasgow apart from Edinburgh is that, if visiting in Glasgow you will instantly be offered tea and cakes, while in the less generous capital you will be asked 'You'll have had your tea already?' Tea has always been an obsession and getting good tea a crucial aspect of life, as this 1910 advert from William Andrew clearly shows. (*UGA*)

Of course, not everyone lived in elegant Victorian town houses and wore the latest fashions. Life at 20 School Wynd off Union Place would have been hard for these children and their dog in 1912. Today, the site is a multi-storey car park. (*ML*)

Sanitation, too, was a hit-or-miss affair in the Glasgow slums. Ashpits like these were common in 1912. In fact, Glasgow prided itself on its sewerage and refuse collection systems, but for a wholly practical reason – this (and the prospect of police protection) were the main arguments used to persuade the wealthy suburbs to come under the umbrella of Greater Glasgow at this time. This young denizen of the centre's slums might well ask 'Where's mine, then?' (*ML*)

But at least someone took the rubbish away. This surprised dustman of 1910, unused to flashlight photography, is doubtless on the verge of delivering a pithy epithet to summarise what he thinks of the photographer and his new-fangled equipment, creeping up on decent folk like that. (*ML*)

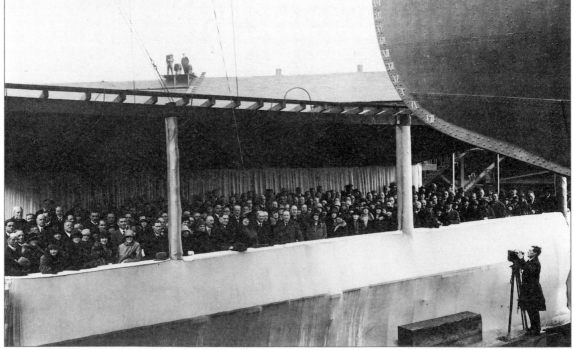

And was this the photographer? Someone had to take these pictures, but it is unusual to see a photographer in a photo. This one, at Napier & Miller's yard in 1911, seems more interested in the launch party than the huge vessel above him. (*UGA*)

The End of
the Good Times

Preparing for war, the Hillhead Officer Training Corps and the Glasgow Academy Officer Training Corps are on Church Parade at Camp Barry in 1914. How many of these young men went to the trenches, and how many returned, is not known. (*UGA*)

In the first half of the twentieth century Glasgow was the centre of Britain's munitions industry, supplying arms and ships for the two world wars. By 1914 naval munitions had become a speciality in its own right, as these gun mountings on the battleships *Barham* and *Repulse* show. The *Barham* took part in the Battle of Jutland as part of 5th Battle Squadron, carrying Rear-Admiral Evan-Thomas. (*UGA*)

The battle-cruiser HMS *Repulse* left the Clyde to join Admiral Tovey's fleet at Scapa Flow alongside HMS *King George V*, a sister ship of HMS *Prince of Wales*, the aircraft-carrier HMS *Victorious*, four cruisers and seven destroyers. HMS *Repulse*, coming from the Clyde, joined them later. The *Bismarck* was sunk and the war at sea decided. On 10 December 1941 the Royal Navy suffered their greatest single loss as a result of a single engagement, when the *Prince of Wales* and *Repulse* were sunk by Japanese warplanes 50 miles off the coast of Kuantan in Malaya, with the loss of over 840 officers and men. (*UGA*)

Springburn Hospital at Stobhill was a major centre for recuperation and convalescence. The grim reality of the war for the wounded soldiers must have been a stark contrast to this rather cheery 1915 postcard of the hospital recreation room. (*ML*)

The steady recruitment of young men continued unabated into the war years. This 1916 picture records the much-expanded Hillhead OTC. (*UGA*)

Glasgow tenements were now a feature of the landscape, some of them erected by the equivalent of today's housing associations. This 1915 back view of Glasgow Workmen's Dwelling House Co. houses is in the inelegantly named Rottenrow. (*ML*)

Lloyd George attended a meeting at St Andrew's Hall on Christmas Day 1915. He hoped to rally trade union support by arguing for the necessary end to strict skills demarcations in the all-out battle to win the race to produce naval ships. Despite his oratory and some outright flattery – 'the Scots have only got one bad fault: there are too few of them', he declaimed – he failed to win over his audience. The meeting broke up in disarray. Regardless, the government later passed legislation to impose mandatory 'skills dilution', women and unskilled workers taking jobs previously reserved for engineers and craftsmen. Strikes at works including Beardmore's in 1916 threatened the war effort, and shop stewards held responsible were exiled to Edinburgh for the duration, under the Defence of the Realm Act, on the premise that they could do less damage outside the Clyde Munitions area. However, the tradition of 'Red Clydeside' had started. (*UGA*)

Women found war work easier to get after the full effects of the Clyde Dilution Commission were felt. Here, they are making grenades at the Elmbank Foundry in Possil Road, 1916. (*ML*)

Apart from taking on skilled and semi-skilled work, women also found entry into what had previously been considered 'men-only' occupations – such as here, doing foundry work and machining at Stephens. Women were a crucial part of the workforce throughout the war period. (*UGA*)

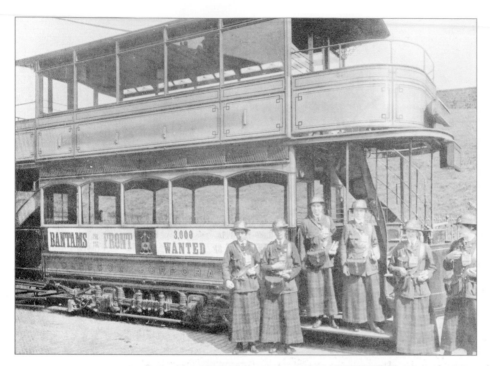

Women found jobs in many other areas of work left vacant by men away at the Front. The first women tram conductresses were seen, and became objects of great, if wary, affection. Their strict control of seating and ticketing on busy, loaded trams was legendary. 'If half o' yez got aff, there wid be room for a' o' yez' is but one recorded pearl of wisdom from these stalwarts of the transport system. (*ML*)

Other than that, life went on as usual in other endeavours, as this self-satisfied portrait of the Glasgow Football Association committee, 1917–18, shows. But while the war effort was continuing, two opposing forces were about to clash over what would be a struggle for control of Glasgow's means of production and economy. The business elite which dominated local government, as well as organisations like the Football Association, would meet head on with the Independent Labour movement and the new trade unions. (*ML*)

Between the Wars

Murray's newsagents (then Murray & Grant), in Byres Road next to the Curler's Tavern, now an off-licence. Notice the looming awareness in 1919 of over-population, the price of food and the financial well-being of Glasgow. (*UGA*)

The story of twentieth-century Glasgow after the First World War is in stark contrast to the previous century, with industrial decline of enormous proportions. There is still work at this paint shop at the Cowlairs works in 1920, but this was not to last. Almost 100,000 people were out of work by 1922. (*ML*)

'The price o' funerals these days, it's cheaper to stay alive', was a music hall joke of the day. Although expensive, with the hearse to rent, funeral director to pay and a ham tea to provide for the sudden rush of distant cousins and long-lost friends among the mourners, 'having a decent send-off' was the aim of every right-thinking Glaswegian. A good funeral, like this one outside the premises of John Smart, a grain dealer in Garscube Road, Port Dundas, in 1920, could be guaranteed to attract a large group of adults and children. (*ML*)

Pleasure cruises 'Doon the watter' or to the islands became an extremely popular Glasgow pastime. McBrayne's *Grenadier*, seen here taking passengers to Iona, had spent the war as a minesweeper and later operated on the Oban–Iona and Gourock–Ardrishaig routes. She caught fire at Oban in 1927. (*UGA*)

Child health was a growing concern and many new agencies and centres sprang up to deal with the increasing awareness. Cochrane Street Child Welfare Clinic was a well-known venue for mothers and children. (*ML*)

At Mount Vernon Day Nursery, children were fed and cared for while mothers worked. Mount Vernon is still in existence as a playgroup. (*ML*)

Glasgow Electric Theatre, 49–55 Argyle Street, was a popular early cinema in 1922. (*ML*)

By the next year times were proving harder and harder for the cinema now known as the Argyle Electric Theatre. (*ML*)

The proposed cinema at the Botanic Gardens never got completed in the atmosphere of austerity which permeated the mid-1920s. (*UGA*)

The State Cinema, however, did get built in the Shettleston Road, in a style far different from the Victorian buildings of the city centre. (*ML*)

The launch of the Cunard liners *Queen Mary* and *Queen Elizabeth* remained proud moments for Glasgow, and 'Clyde-built' still meant quality. Yorkhill Dock, shown in this aerial view of the east basin, was a major berth for these and other ships. (*ML*)

Finnieston Quay at Anderston was busy in the 1930s. Rearmament of the navy before and during the Second World War and the need to replace lost vessels afterwards stayed the industrial decline to an extent. But trade barriers, disarmament agreements and the growing threat of emerging ship-building industries overseas combined to make the outlook gloomy. (*ML*)

D. & W. Henderson's Meadowside shipyard, Partick, 1930. Glasgow was still recovering from the effects of the 1926 General Strike, and there had been a fall in shipbuilding output from 670,000 tons in 1920 to a disastrously low 175,000 tons in 1923, although it had risen again to the previous level by the time this picture was taken. (*ML*)

Glasgow had already diversified its industry away from shipping alone, as the 1930s St Rollox Chemical Works shows. This had started when Charles Macintosh (of waterproof garment fame) and Charles Tennant invented a process for bleaching textiles. Tennant opened his works in the early nineteenth century and was soon producing, in addition to bleaching salt, sulphuric acid, soap, soda and fertiliser. The famous 'Tennant's Stalk' or 'St Rollox Lum', a 500 ft chimney, was a landmark and signal of his achievement. The pollution was horrendous. Tennant also helped to found the steel industry, by applying his chemical skills to the search for an alternative to pig-iron. (*ML*)

Charing Cross from
the west, Sauchiehall
Street, 1926. (*ML*)

Boots in Burleigh Street, Govan, had a new shopfront in 1927. (*ML*)

The Springburn works were, by 1930, largely turning out locomotive engines, such as these North British engines being transported through the streets. (*ML*)

Successive waves of Italian immigrants bolstered the multicultural life of Glasgow in the early part of the century. By the 1930s many were in their third generations, such as the Crollas and Gizzis. Ice-cream was a way of life for Glaswegians and ice-cream making a high art, as these prizes testify. (*ML*)

Of course, it's one thing to make ice-cream but another to persuade people into shops and cafés to buy it. The alternative? The ice-cream cart, like Notarianni's 1930s horse-drawn van. (*ML*)

Art Gallery and Museum, Kelvingrove, 1930. Grand Victorian public buildings had been constructed and many of Glasgow's wealthier citizens spent their fortunes on amassing the large art collections which now form the basis of the city's excellent galleries. The impressive central hall is dominated at one end by organ pipes (recitals are an integral part of the museum programme) and the art gallery upstairs houses the city's collection of nineteenth- and twentieth-century works. Scottish painters are comprehensively represented as are Rembrandt, Botticelli, Monet, Van Gogh and Picasso. (*ML*)

Glasgow Cross Tolbooth at the Trongate, 1930. The cross was the heart of Glasgow until 1800, when people and businesses started to move west. High Street leads to the medieval cathedral and the original site of the university, which left for the more spacious Gilmorehill in 1870. The southern route led to the Saltmarket and Briggat ('Bridge Gate'), west was Trongate (shown here) and the road east headed for the Gallowgate. The predominance of 'Gate' names shows the early origin of most of these. The Tolbooth steeple continues to frustrate traffic planners who would dearly love to flatten it. (*ML*)

Barclays' Tearoom was typical of the 1930s. (*UGA*)

Murray's, in Byres Road, continued to provide news, fags and chocolate to the West End citizenry. Mr Baldwin's speech was clearly the main selling point. Today Byres Road is still considered 'the main artery through the heart of the city' – cosmopolitan, multi-cultured, bohemian, intellectual, grand, leafy, confident, tolerant and 'trendy'. (*UGA*)

Policeman William Hughes on duty at the Botanic Gardens. When he joined the force Hillhead had been an independent police burgh. These were all annexed to the city by 1912. (*UGA*)

Aerial view from Port Dundas westwards, 1937. Port Dundas grew as the Forth & Clyde canal developed, which linked Greenock to Leith near Edinburgh. It became a centre for grain mills, chemical works, dye shops, distilleries and other enterprises which depended on water and water transport. It was home to William Burrell's 'puffer' shipyard which later diversified into ship-owning, evidently successfully as the works of art he amassed were later to become the Burrell Collection. (*ML*)

Possibly in an attempt to win back its overseas markets and strengthen its ties with the former colonies, Glasgow staged the Empire Exhibition in 1938. This aerial view of the expo site in Bellahouston Park and the one below show the scale of the exercise. (*ML*)

Sited in one of Glasgow's largest municipal parks, the main theme was energy, ranging from sports demonstrations to the Palace of Engineering and a temporary Butlin's. Like its modern counterpart, the Millennium Dome in Greenwich, it had disappointing attendance figures – 12.5 million instead of the expected 20 million. The weather was blamed, and the need to close on Sundays couldn't have helped either. (*ML*)

The spectacular Tait Tower in Bellahouston Park was the showpiece of the 1938 Empire Exhibition. Thomas Tait intended the 100-yard-high tower to be a symbol of modernism, and this and the other exhibition architecture was hailed as innovatory. (*ML*)

The Second World War

Sir Winston Churchill inspecting air raid wardens, 1941. On another occasion he wrote: 'Of all the small nations of this earth, perhaps only the ancient Greeks surpass the Scots in their contribution to mankind.' (*ML*)

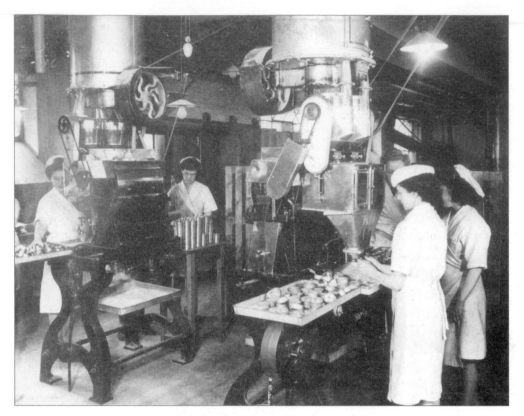

All production turned towards helping the war effort, even the venerable 'Co-op'. Women again found war work, in this case at the Scottish Cooperative Wholesale Society (SCWS) in Shieldhall, packing tea, milk and sugar tablets for rations. (*ML*)

Another aspect of SCWS war work was the use of its sheet metal factory to produce bombs, here seen leaving the factory in Shieldhall in 1942. (*ML*)

Despite the war there was work again, and the desire to spend wages on entertainment. 'Ra Dancin' was an important aspect of social life for young Glasgow. Famous venues included the Top Hat Ballroom above these shops in Pollokshaws Road, Shawlands. (*ML*)

Another centre of terpsichorean diversion was the F & F Palais de Danse in Dumbarton Road, Partick. (*ML*)

Before Archaos, Cathouse and The Tunnel, the Barrowland Ballroom on Gallowgate was the original and is still considered to be the best music venue in Scotland. The famous Barrowland Market ('Ra Barras') is still the weekend secondhand and bric-a-brac mecca. It is largely unchanged from this 1940 photograph, apart from the garish posters which now decorate its exterior. (*ML*)

A marked departure from the typical ground-floor shopfronts Glaswegians were used to, new single-storey shops were the coming style in the 1940s. These paramount examples of functionality over elegance are at Smithycroft Road, Riddrie. (*ML*)

Even existing shops bowed to the new style of large window fronts, ruining many a street's harmonious look and integrity. This picture shows 344–52 Dumbarton Road, Partick. (*ML*)

More welcoming, but still with an eye to security and defence of property, is this typical refit of 769 Springburn Road in May 1940. It may be coincidental that women were to be found serving in pubs for the first time since a temperance law passed in 1902. The formidable Glasgow barmaid was again a fixture. (*ML*)

As life returned to normal after the war some places were changed forever. Sauchiehall Street had adopted the new, garish style. (*ML*)

The full employment provided by war work was disappearing, and unemployed men were again seen on street corners, like this one at Cowcaddens. (*ML*)

Shipyard work usually lasted from 6 am to 5 pm, with a half day on Saturday, after which it was football. The sheer numbers employed on one project can be seen, as they leave HMS *Hood* after a day's shift, and every single one dressed like Paw Broon. The wartime bounty lasted after 1945, as new ships had to be commissioned and older ones refitted. (*UGA*)

Many Glasgow tenements had been provided with air raid precautions such as these back-green shelters. Glasgow had not been hit as badly as Clydebank, where over 30,000 inhabitants were rendered homeless in two nights in 1941. None the less, some bomb damage, deteriorating housing stock, an organised squat campaign by the homeless and a plague of rats combined to increase the pressure on Glasgow Corporation to address the housing issue, and make tenements such as these a thing of the past. (*ML*)

After the War

PC William Joyner served Hillhead from 1950 to 1962, and saw the immense changes to Glasgow which took place after the war. (*UGA*)

As part of the Corporation's new-found desire to sort out the housing situation, sewer cutting began in the Shettleston Road in 1949. This was a component of the Bruce Plan, a fifty-year programme of modernisation aimed at combining housing redevelopment and civic monumentalism which argued against relocation of the population to a planned New Town outside Glasgow's boundaries and for tenement renovation, high-rises in garden suburbs and – above all – keeping taxpayers within the city limits. Robert Bruce, the City Engineer, whose 1945 and 1946 reports had formed the basis of this ambitious scheme, was outflanked and outgunned by Patrick Abercrombie, fresh from the success of his Greater London Plan. He played the 'Greater Glasgow' card, which appealed to the aspirations of some of the councillors. (*ML*)

Corporation housing also improved inside. In 1952, when this picture was taken, half of Glasgow dwellings had no fixed bath and over a third had a shared toilet. Stunning luxury and convenience were embodied in the type T1/4 interior seen here at 42 Parkneuk Road, Mansewood. (*ML*)

The new architecture which was to dominate Glasgow's cityscape is typified by these 1950 views of the west side of Kilmarnock Road, Shawlands. These photographs are taken from 151 Kilmarnock Road with a view of the aptly named White Elephant Cinema. (*ML*)

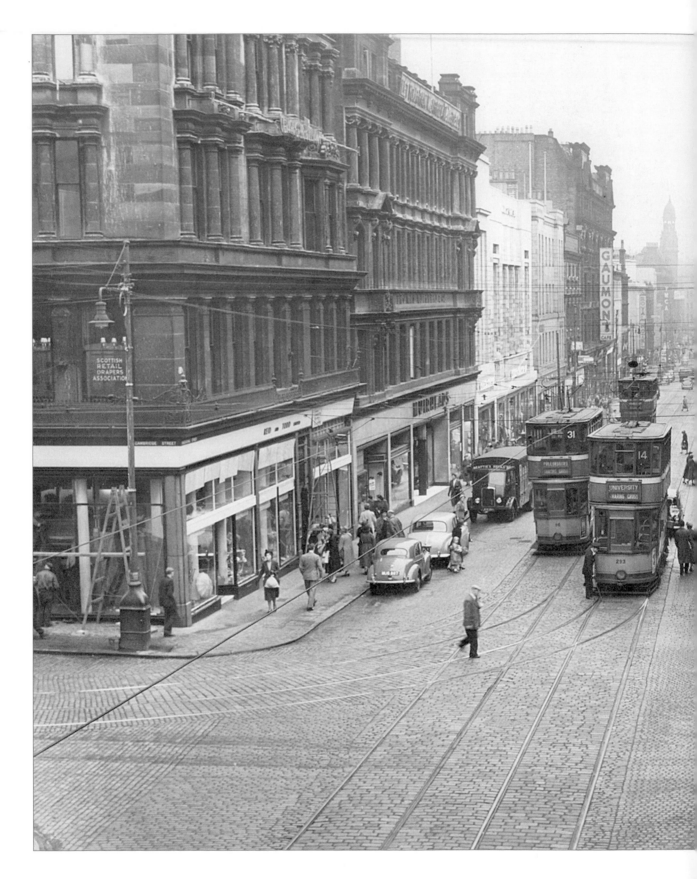

Sauchiehall Street, looking east from Cambridge Street, c. 1950. By this time the shops 'as fine as any in Bond Street' had mostly gone, swept away by an advancing tide of chain stores which continued to proliferate in the 1960s. The touchstone of Glasgow retailing excellence, Copland and Lye, followed. Plans to turn either Sauchiehall Street or Buchanan Street into a Champs Elysées never materialised, the effort instead going into malls. (ML)

Much of the pre-war feel of Glasgow was vanishing fast by 1950. But even if hemlines were rising to immoderate heights, the staff at Hunter's at Victoria Cross still wore aprons and the managers dark suits. (*UGA*)

It was a common jest in the early 1950s that the Cleansing Department's horses deposited more refuse than their carts took away. This horse parade shows how well decked-out these fine animals were. The scavengers, or scaffies, as they were known, first emerged at the beginning of the nineteenth century as Glasgow took responsibility for its garbage collection, as well as its fire brigade and police services. (*ML*)

The Queen, the Duke of Edinburgh and Provost
Thomas A. Kerr visited Hampden in 1953. Her
Majesty seems blissfully unaware that Sir Basil
Spence's prize-winning Queen Elizabeth flats,
then being erected in the Gorbals, were named
not after her royal self, but the ocean liner
whose design he took as his inspiration. Still,
she probably enjoyed the game and had a
Bovril. (*ML*)

Equally as elegant as the
young Queen, 5 Blythswood
Square was formerly the
home of the Glasgow Society
of Lady Artists, now renamed
the less high-sounding
Glasgow Society of Women
Artists. This Rennie
Mackintosh building can be
viewed from the exterior only,
but it holds many gems, such
as this fireplace,
photographed in 1955. (*ML*)

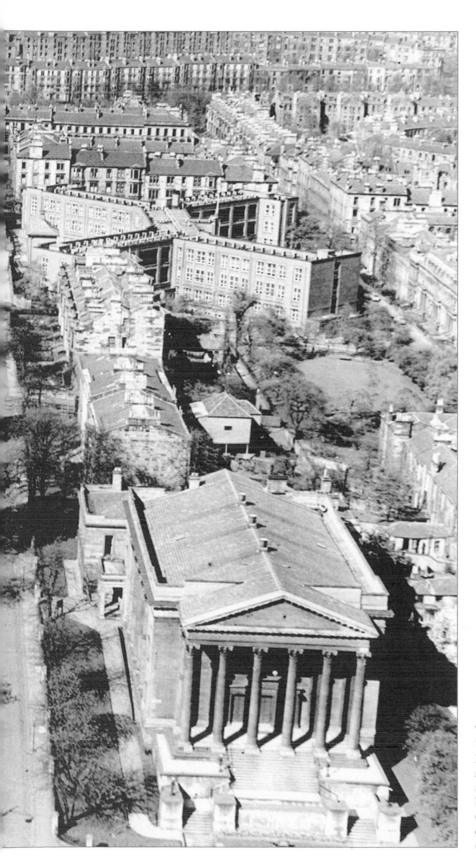

This 1950s view north from the University Tower over the Reading Room and Wellington Church shows that Glasgow had tree-lined avenues, elegant circuses and fine buildings to rival any capital city. Concrete high-rises were not yet in evidence, but were not far away. (*UGA*)

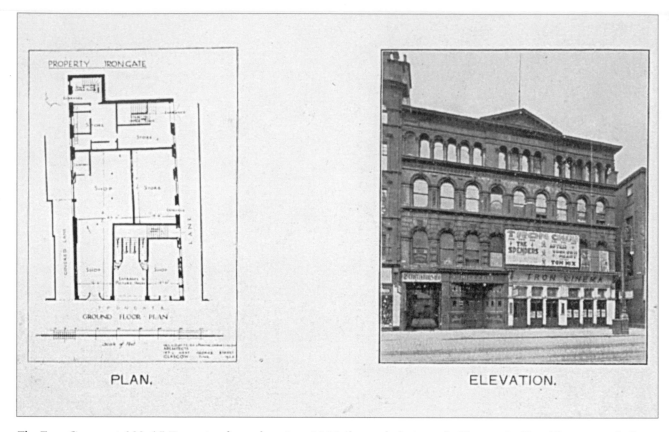

PLAN.   ELEVATION.

The Tron Cinema at 109–15 Trongate, shown here in a 1955 plan and photograph. The nearby Tron Theatre was built on the site of the old Tron church, a 1590s building which burnt down during a drunken spree by the Hellfire Club in 1793. A new church was constructed, but it had been left roofless for years. (*ML*)

From the Trongate and right at The Cross, off Saltmarket, is St Andrew's Square, site of the former City Orphanage Working Boys' Home. (*ML*)

Miller's shop at 182 Trongate was one of those which resisted modernisation. (*ML*)

It was often said that more drunks were arrested in Hope Street (pictured here in 1946) than in neighbouring Sauchiehall Street, not because it was inherently a worse place, but because policemen found it easier to spell, and dragged their arrestees there in order to book them. That aside, it was, and remains, one of Glasgow's more characterful thoroughfares. (*ML*)

Kelvinside was by 1955 fully part of Glasgow, in marked distinction to its earlier status as a slightly snooty, stand-offish consumer of Glaswegian amenities such as parks and gardens, without contributing to the upkeep. Lansdowne church in Great Western Road, seen here, is now a popular venue for concerts, and boasts one of the best pipe organs in Scotland. (*ML*)

By contrast, the back court of Adelphi Street in the Gorbals, also photographed in 1955, shows that not all city residents lived in tree-lined elegance. (*ML*)

Albion Motors represents what remains of the Scottish automotive industry. The Albion Motor Works in Scotstoun, shown here in 1955, was founded in 1899 as the Albion Motor Car Co. and survives today as Albion Automotive, which supplies truck and van parts. By 1903 car and light van production was taking place in a 42,000 sq. ft factory. In 1951 Albion was the first acquisition of Leyland Motors (later British Leyland), and by 1960 the Glasgow plant was designing and producing axles and transmission systems for other Leyland companies. In 1980 Albion ceased vehicle production in favour of its axle range. Leyland's interests were acquired by DAF, which collapsed in 1993 leaving the British concerns in receivership. From these ashes Albion Automotive was formed; Volvo's Farington plant was acquired in 1995 and the company continues to produce axles in Glasgow. (*ML*)

Glasgow had long had a tradition of locomotive engineering, starting with Henry Dubs' Polmadie works in 1865. The North British Locomotive Company, formed in 1903 from smaller manufacturers, was the largest engine makers in the world outside the USA. This photograph shows an engine from Hyde Park Locomotive Works, Springburn, passing under the canal in 1955. (*ML*)

Never let it be said that Glasgow can't enjoy itself, though. The fair in Glasgow Green is a long-standing tradition, dating back to the annual market established in the twelfth century. Although there was a hiatus after evangelical temperance bodies managed to have it moved to Camlachie, citing it to be 'one large brothel' and a 'source of evil', it was again in full swing by 1955, as can be seen here. (*ML*)

Dog racing at Shawfield Park was another diversion of the 1950s. Bear in mind that Glasgow's sabbatarian and temperance spoilsports had conspired to keep music and sports out of the public parks on Sundays until fairly recently, and that as late as the 1950s a gentle game of bowls was denied on the Sabbath. What heights of fury, then, must the Holy Wullies have been driven to by seeing people take honest enjoyment and a modest wager at 'The Dugs'. (*ML*)

Even better than a decent funeral, Glaswegians enjoy a good wedding. This happy couple tying the knot at St Agnes' Church, Balmore Road, Possilpark, in 1955 will soon be planning their golden anniversary. (*ML*)

Argyle Street holds a special place in the hearts of true Glasgow folk – much more so than the better known Sauchiehall Street. Originally the Yoker Turnpike, it is fully 2 miles long, from the Trongate to the River Kelvin. The eastern end is well known for its shops, notably Lewis's and the Anderston Centre (a planners' fantasy) but the quieter, leafier western part is home to the Kelvin Hall and the art galleries. Even on this dreich day in 1957 it has a certain quiet charm. (*ML*)

Kelvingrove Park in the 1950s. (*UGA*)

It seems that almost every seaport in Britain has a King George V Dock, but Glasgow's is something special. Shipbuilding had seen a resurgence in the early 1950s. Many potential competitor countries were still rebuilding their economies and the Korean War came along just as the refitting wave of the Second World War was fading. Unemployment was low (in complete contrast to the disastrous time immediately prior to 1938). Some 15 per cent of the workforce was in engineering and metal industries, including shipbuilding, and a further 11 per cent, mainly women, in the clerical posts which underpinned the commercial economy. Workers were needed, too, for the vast housing schemes being built in and around the city. But although an annual figure of 400,000 tonnes of new shipping launched annually in the 1950s sounds impressive, it represented less than 5 per cent of the world's tonnage, while pre-1914 Glasgow had been used to commanding 20 per cent. The fear of nationalisation prompted overseas investment and hampered inward investment. Planning laws aimed to move large industry away from city centres to New Towns, and Glasgow then had no motorway system. This shipworker seems to recognise the oncoming recession in 1957. However, the dock has seen a new lease of life forty years on. John R. Adam & Sons carry out metal processing and exporting from a riverside site which can accommodate large ships. The Glasgow and Renfrew District Railway has a station there. And recently Clydeport plc, Scotland's west coast port operator, trumpeted the news of the largest vessel to berth in the upper reaches of the Glasgow harbour area in over ten years – the 230 metres long *Alexandropolis*, loaded with 37,000 tonnes of grain for Saudi Arabia. Perhaps it isn't all gone, after all. (*ML*)

A much loved figure, John Jones, the Punch & Judy Professor, who toured the West End with his brother before and after the First World War, died in 1960 aged sixty-eight, soon after this photograph was taken. (*UGA*)

Scots Guards marching through the city and back to Kelvingrove Park in 1959 could still command a large crowd. (*UGA*)

Workers leaving the Twomax factory, Rutherglen Road, Hutchesontown, in July 1956 would be aghast if they knew that the old mill building was now the home of Glasgow's Community Adolescent Psychiatry service. (*ML*)

If anything could sum up the feeling of a new era just around the corner, it is this picture of the young staff of a nationalised industry (South of Scotland Electricity Board) doing the twist during a pleasure cruise in 1958. Teenagers had been invented, Rock'n'Roll was here to stay and the 1960s were almost upon us. (*ML*)

Building the Future
over the Past

St Mungo, patron saint of Glasgow, looks out at Kelvingrove Art Gallery in
the 1960s, a scant 1,400 years after he and his mother, St Thenew (or
St Enoch), established their episcopal church at nearby Molendinar. (*UGA*)

Hillington Industrial Estate had been a pioneering exercise in the 1930s. The ideas tested in Welwyn Garden City, Slough and elsewhere – light industrial units, grants and rates rebates – were adopted. Although they employed few (5,000 by 1939) they had notable PR successes. Hillington was the source of the Penguin biscuit and later Rolls-Royce aero engines. Women workers recruited there complained about low wages and discrimination and, unusually for wartime, went on strike and won. The Hillington venture survived into the 1960s, and continues to thrive. (*ML*)

Shieldhall Wharf also continued to operate, despite a global recession in shipping, which hit Glasgow harder than many places not so monolithically dependent. In 1961 Glasgow looked longingly at the subsidies and assistance handed out in West Germany, Sweden and Holland. (*ML*)

A sign of the times: this horse-drawn tram leads the final procession of electric tramcars of earlier periods on 4 September 1962, bringing to an end this world famous transport system. (*UGA*)

Sights like this 1960 view of the Hyndland Road terminus and the interior view of the Woodlands Road tramcar (below) were now a memory. (*UGA*)

Some still clung to the old ways throughout the 1960s, like this rag and bone man at Eldon Street Bridge. (*UGA*)

Meanwhile, the increased access to higher education meant enormous growth in Glasgow University student numbers. This 1963 Rag Day parade in North Street, Anderston, shows typical high spirits. (*ML*)

The world was still ill-divided, though. These children at the rear of their Cowcaddens tenement in 1963 could only dream of West End or Southside houses. But social changes were coming fast which would sweep away the old class barriers. (*ML*)

Bute Gardens, near the university and Kelvingrove, was undergoing changes throughout the decade, as this 1965 construction site shows. (*UGA*)

Around the corner, Lilybank Gardens was also having its bumps felt. This 1968 photograph shows the site of the new Boyd Orr building. (*UGA*)

Did Lord Provost Victor Warren know, in his home in Bute Gardens, that the area around him would soon see terraces swept away, to be replaced by high-rise office buildings? Presumably his planning department kept him informed. Note the bailie's lamp outside his door. (*UGA*)

It had been typical for bailies (senior elected councillors) to have a special gas lamp erected outside their homes, such as this one in Otago Street, so that the public would know where they lived. This custom is now gone in most Scottish cities, for reasons of cost and also because there is now no guarantee that a bailie won't live twenty storeys up in a block of flats, rather than in an elegant town house. (*UGA*)

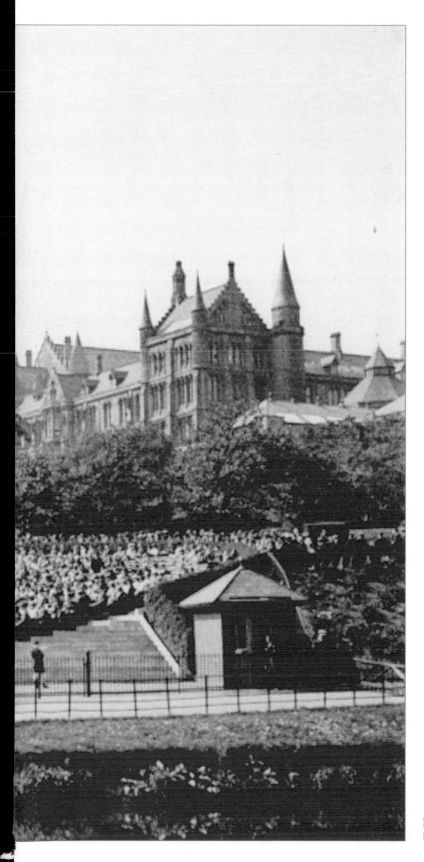

Kelvingrove Park and Park Terrace, with Glasow
University behind, in the 1960s. (*UGA*)

Some things never change. Children will play in the streets, like these in Anderston in 1961, unaware that their house will be a multi-storey car park by the time they come to look for housing of their own. (*ML*)

Mr Stott's milk cart was still a common sight around Hillhead in the 1960s. (*UGA*)

The 1870s had seen a great surge of school building in the wake of the 1872 Education Act, which brought schools under the control of elected boards – although the Catholic schools stayed outwith the system. One third of the seventy-five new schools constructed between 1874 and 1916 were built in a six-year period. One such was Tureen Street Occupational Centre (1876) in Calton, shown here in 1964. (ML)

The new housing of the '50s and '60s also demanded new schools, and these were not built in the same high style as those ninety years earlier. Miltonbank Primary in Possil serves the community in the new flats behind. (ML)

Bingo was fast becoming the new religion. The Astoria Bingo Club at the corner of Possil Road and Bairds Brae is typical of the breed, pictured here in 1964. (*ML*)

The same year parts of India Street in Charing Cross were being demolished in the interests of the new modernism. Would Greek Thomson have approved? (*ML*)

Glasgow's underground stations were also due for a much-needed facelift. Buchanan Street station is almost unrecognisable today from this 1964 picture. (*UGA*)

The same is true of Kelvinbridge station, shown here in 1965. (*UGA*)

This aerial view of Prince's Dock, Govan, in 1965 was taken at the height of the Wilson government's intervention in the disastrous decline of Glasgow's shipping industry. The Fairfield Yard had just collapsed and a new consortium was formed to stave off the worst. Two combines emerged as a result of the Geddes Report in 1966 – Scott-Lithgow in Greenock and Upper Clyde Shipbuilders (UCS) in Glasgow and Clydebank. There was little harmony between the UCS members, even if occasional high points like the *QEII* helped. (*ML*)

But there was always Auntie Beeb. The BBC had broadcast from Glasgow since 1923 under the watchful if distant eye of John Reith, a native of the city. Television arrived in 1952. The BBC Radio headquarters were Cranworth House in 1968. (*UGA*)

The Lost Empire

This Partick coalman is probably thinking, 'Here we are in 1970, but people will always need coal delivered.' Oh, really? (*UGA*)

The Botanic Gardens station suffered a destructive fire in 1970. Fortunately a rebuilding programme for Glasgow's transport was under way, although this station was not rebuilt. (*UGA*)

These buildings in Ashton Lane, Byres Road, were demolished for a new subway station in 1972. (*UGA*)

Finally, Glasgow got its motorway. For all the purists complain about the huge concrete scar across the city and the destruction of much of St George's Cross to make way for it, there is no question it has improved movement into, out of and within the city. This 1971 view shows the new M8 at Pinkston, just before it enters Cowcaddens. (*ML*)

Some landmarks continued to disappear. The demolition of the Cleansing Department chimney, south of Yorkhill Hospital in 1973, was a *cause célèbre* at the time. (*ML*)

If anything improved the mood at this time, apart from better transport, it was the 1976 relaxation of licensing laws. The temperance movement had forced various draconian strictures on Glasgow from 1890 onwards, including no alcohol in council housing. This led to entire housing schemes with no watering hole nearby and resulted in the establishment of illegal stills and shebeens all over the city. This, together with the 10 pm closing, no Sunday drinking except in hotels for 'bona fide travellers' and the general drink-it-and-leave atmosphere in many pubs led directly to Glaswegians' reputation for disputatious drunkenness. This is the Buck's Head in Argyle Street. (*ML*)

Another pub in Argyle Street, The Shandon, was due for a facelift as reconstruction happened around it in 1975. The children presumably found somewhere else to play. (*ML*)

Rebuilding happened too. The High Court in Glasgow Green's Saltmarket, built by William Stark in 1807, was rebuilt in 1971, retaining the stunning portico. (*ML*)

Clean air had had a remarkable effect on the exteriors of central Glasgow's elegant buildings. For the first time in a century the true mellow sandstone colour was seen again. Other beautification occurred at the same time, as witness this image of James Salmon's 1906 Lion Chambers at 172 Hope Street, 1975. (*ML*)

Glasgow had had two universities since the creation of Strathclyde in 1964 (pictured here in 1979) and would receive another in 1993 when Glasgow Caledonian received Incorporated status along with other UK polytechnics and their Scottish equivalents, the central institutions. While these last have still to prove their mettle, Strathclyde has nothing to be insecure about, having steadily built a world-class reputation over the past forty years. (*ML*)

Entertainment comes in many guises. The Apollo Centre in Renfield Street found a role for itself as a major concert venue, getting ready here for the 1978 David Bowie Stage Tour. (*ML*)

Others preferred the gentler pursuits of equestrianism and football, seen here in fine combination as mounted policemen encourage the crowds, probably at Hampden. (*ML*)

Some like to run . . . (Glasgow Marathon, on the Expressway near Yorkhill Quay, 1983). (*ML*)

. . . while others prefer to walk (Orange Parade at the corner of Crow Road and Dumbarton Road, July 1996). Glasgow has lost much of the bigotry which typified, for instance, the 1920s and 1930s, when the Protestant Billy Boys would slog it out with their Catholic rivals from Norman Street, the Norman Conquerors. But feelings still run deep. (*ML*)

The Next Century

Glasgow in the twenty-first century: Brian Allen's impression of the Glasgow Science Centre with the city beyond. The Glasgow tower has 521 steps in its staircase – but most visitors will use the rack-and-pinion lifts, which will take two-and-a-half minutes to reach the 104-metre high viewing cabin. (*GSC*)

Glasgow also has high hopes for the new Science Centre at Pacific Quay, on the site of the 1988 Garden Festival. The picture below, taken in July 2000, shows the GSC complex from across Princes Dock. The base of the tower is extreme left, with the developing Science Mall in the middle and the IMAX theatre on the right. (*ML above; GSC below*)

The famous Finnieston crane provides an aerial view of the Seamen's Restaurant, a marked contrast to The Armadillo (Clyde Auditorium), the new 3,000-seat venue at the Scottish Exhibition and Conference Centre. The crane still stands and 'Glasgow's answer to the Sydney Opera House' hulks alongside. (*ML*)

The IMAX theatre at the Science Centre. (*GSC*)

The Armadillo by day and night. (*Scottish Enterprise Glasgow*)

The Forth & Clyde Canal – Linking the Oceans. The Millennium Link is a £78m project which will restore the Forth & Clyde and Union Canals to their former glory, making them fully navigable for the first time in almost forty years by Easter 2001. The Forth & Clyde Canal was the world's first man-made sea-to-sea ship canal and connected Edinburgh and Glasgow. The project is predicted to assist in creating over 4,000 new full-time jobs across Central Scotland.

The idea for a canal to link the Atlantic and what was then called the 'German Ocean' (the North Sea) was first suggested in the time of Charles II as a passage for warships. In the early eighteenth century several surveys were undertaken, which attracted the support of, among others, Daniel Defoe and architect William Adam. Unusually, the estimated costs for building the canal went down rather than up from the late seventeenth-century figure of £500,000 to £80,000 in 1760. In 1763 the Board of Trustees for the Encouragement of Fisheries, Manufactures & Improvements in Scotland appointed Yorkshire engineer John Smeaton to survey the route. Smeaton's proposals provoked outrage among the Glasgow Tobacco merchants as it bypassed the city. They commissioned a rival survey, from Robert Mackell and James Watt. At this time the Clyde was only 4 ft deep in Glasgow and bringing the canal into the city centre would have limited its depth and usefulness. Edinburgh dismissed the Glasgow counter-proposals as 'a ditch, a gutter, a mere puddle' which would do nothing for 'magnificence and national honour': 'The fools of the West must wait for the Wise Men of the East.' The proponents of a 'grand canal' won and Smeaton revised his plans, taking a 7 ft-draught canal into the Clyde at Dalmuir and suggesting a branch into Glasgow. The canal was 35 miles long, with an additional 3½ miles on the branch into Port Dundas in Glasgow; 60 ft wide and 9 ft deep, it rose to 156 feet above sea level, through twenty locks on the eastern side and nineteen on the western. The Kelvin Aqueduct built to carry it was the largest of its kind in Britain and the area behind it became known as Butney, after Botany Bay, because convict labour was used. It opened in July 1790 but gave way to the railway in 1867.

In 1948 the canal was taken over by the British Transport Commission and then, in 1962, by the British Waterways Board. If the railways sounded its death knell, road transport delivered the killing blow. It was decided to close the canal rather than invest £160,000 in building a lift bridge at the Denny bypass on the Glasgow–Stirling road. All rights to navigation ceased on 1 January 1963.

Acknowledgements

Images marked UGA were kindly provided by and are reproduced by kind permission of the University of Glasgow Archives and Business Records. Special thanks are due to Simon Bennett, Duty Archivist, for his help, guidance and patience, and to other staff for their diligence.

Images marked ML were kindly provided by and are reproduced by kind permission of Glasgow City Libraries and Archives. Jan McLaughlin of the Glasgow Room, Mitchell Library, deserves a special mention for her assiduity and cooperation.

Thanks are also due to David Grimmer and the Glasgow Science Centre for kind permission to include the images on pages 115, 116 and 119, and to Victoria Fulton and Scottish Enterprise Glasgow for kind permission to use the photographs on page 119.

All other images, unless stated otherwise, are from the author's own collection, or were obtained from public domain sources.

The horses, the trams and the gas lamps are away. Glasgow has changed immeasurably since this picture was taken 100 years ago. Yet much of what made it special remains – particularly the spirit and warmth of the Glaswegians, who made a stranger feet at home while compiling the book. This one's for you, Jimmy! (*UGA*)